M.O.O.S.E.M.U.S.S
For
Millennials

Also by Larkin Spivey

God in the Trenches

Miracles of the American Revolution

Battlefields and Blessings: Stories of Faith and Courage from World War II

Stories of Faith and Courage from the Korean War

Stories of Faith and Courage from the Vietnam War

A Skeptic's Guide to God

A Skeptic's Guide to God Group Study

What Do We Stand For?

M.O.O.S.E.M.U.S.S
for *Millennials*

*Principles of War
for Peace-Loving Young Adults*

Lt. Col. Larkin Spivey USMC (ret)

Xulon Press

Xulon Press
2301 Lucien Way #415
Maitland, FL 32751
407.339.4217
www.xulonpress.com

Unless otherwise indicated, Scripture quotations taken from the *Holy Bible, New International Version* (NIV). Copyright © 1973, 1978, 1984, 2011 by Biblica, Inc.™. Used by permission. All rights reserved.

There are numerous other quotations throughout this work, especially in chapter headings and Appendix C. Most are aprocryphal. Where credit is given to an actual person, unless otherwise indicated, such quotes come from multiple internet sites listing famous quotes and are not original sources.

Cover painting: *Intervention of the Sabine Women*, 1799, by Jacques-Louis David. Depicting a legendary episode in the history of Rome during which Sabine women (perhaps early Millennials) sought peace by placing themselves between Roman and Sabine warriors.

Printed in the United States of America.

ISBN-13: 978-1-5456-7542-7

To Sophie

My Soldier

Table of Contents

Principles for Living xiii

Purpose for Living xvii

A Special Note. xxi

Chapter One
Mass 1

Chapter Two
Objective. 7

Chapter Three
Offensive. 13

Chapter Four
Security 19

Chapter Five
Economy of Force. 25

Chapter Six
Maneuver 31

Chapter Seven
Unity of Command 37

Chapter Eight
Surprise 43

Chapter Nine
Simplicity 47

Summary 53

Appendix A
Spiritual Warfare 57

Appendix B
War on Women 61

Appendix C
Military (and related) Axioms 69

I don't care if it works in practice, does it work in theory?[1]

Principles for Living

About MOOSEMUSS: This is a well-known (within military circles) acronym for remembering the nine Principles of War, which are: **M**ass, **O**bjective, **O**ffensive, **S**ecurity, **E**conomy of Force, **M**aneuver, **U**nity of Command, **S**urprise, and **S**implicity.

These principles are intended to serve as guidelines to thoughtful action in war, and, as a rule, are not meant to be rigidly applied in any particular circumstance. Philosophers and soldiers through the ages have tried their hands in an effort to boil down military wisdom into a few fundamentals such as these. Notable military experts such as Sun Tzu, Machiavelli, Von Clausewitz, J. F. C. Fuller, and many others have offered their own prescriptions. The principles included in MOOSEMUSS, however, have survived for many

---

[1] Lament of an old sociology professor.

decades as the official doctrine of the American military establishment.

About MILLENNIALS: Although this

term appears in the title, I have to confess that I have difficulty sorting out the differences in time span and characteristics of baby boomers, Millennials, Gen X, GenY, Gen Z, and other generations yet unnamed. I am, therefore, using the term Millennial as a general phrase for young adults of every generation. I am happy to include in this group anyone younger than myself, which, according to my reckoning, is a lot of people. This misuse of the term is kind of like an older father confusing the names of his children, and I hope readers can forgive accordingly. More than anything, it seemed to make a catchy title for this book.

Can the principles of war be applied to daily living? It's probably a stretch. As a career military person, educated in a military college, my life has been shaped by many military values and attitudes that are pretty foreign to the average young person today. Nevertheless, I would like to share some of these values in the hope that they might help young people navigate the joys and trials of adulthood in today's world.

In a book titled *Corporate Combat,* author William Peacock, also a former Marine, asserts that a military approach to business affairs could give someone a leg up over people in the civilian world who don't think this way. He states, "Today, the businessperson must operate daily as if the environment is a hostile and war-time situation." [2] Peacock is overstating the issue some-what for my purpose in this book, as I will generally be stressing the more positive use of these principles in dealing with situations in everyday life. However, it is indeed true that there are times when the effort needed to be successful in an important endeavor could well take on the nature of a military campaign. It is also true that we sometimes find ourselves in competitive or confrontational situations where we have to be decisive and even tough—when a military approach may be the very thing needed.

In war, the military strategist's purpose is victory, and the principles of war are brought to bear with this end in mind. In everyday life, our purpose is different from the military strategist, but nevertheless needs to be clearly defined. So, some discussion about *purpose* is in order and follows in the next section.

> *At that time Jesus said, "I praise you, Father, Lord of heaven and earth, because you have hidden these things from the wise and learned, and revealed them to little children."* **Matthew 11:25**

---

[2] Peacock, William G. *Corporate Combat, Military Strategies That Win Business Wars*. New York: Berkley Books, 1986, p. 12-13.

He who fears being conquered is sure of defeat.[3]

Purpose for Living

There is a special part of The Citadel Cadet Prayer that states, "Grant to each of us in his own life a humble heart, a steadfast purpose, and a joyful hope." The steadfast purpose part had something to do with my joining the Marine Corps. My purpose as a Marine was clear and exalted, reflecting a mixture of patriotism and dedication to the defense of my country. This animated my life for many years. When I took off the uniform, however, this kind of purpose became harder to find in the world outside military service.

Finding one's purpose is especially challenging for a young person today in our highly materialistic culture. Thankfully, you don't have to enlist in the military to find your own answer. There is undoubtedly purpose to be found in most walks of life, whether in being a good businessman, teacher, doctor, parent, spouse, or even friend. However, if you find your purpose only in your

[3] Napoleon Bonaparte

profession, or in these other roles, I think you will be disappointed eventually. Job changes, disenchantments, life tragedies, even retirement have ways of making once urgent career endeavors seem less important.

What I am suggesting is the idea of an *ultimate* purpose that is transcendent and enduring. And here we have to consider what is *ultimately* important—which has to be, and can only be, the Creator of the universe. Many of my readers are okay with this assertion, but I know that many are not. I am also afraid that some who are okay now may experience later what my daughter calls the "quarter-life crisis," in which the culture turns the beliefs of a young adult (plus or minus 25 years old) upside down.

I accepted Jesus Christ as Lord later in life and finally found that ultimate purpose that comes from the source of life itself. When asked what the greatest commandment is, Jesus replied that we should love God and our neighbors as ourselves,[4] a compelling and challenging purpose reflecting God's love for us. It is in fact a very difficult purpose to live out. In view of our fallen nature as human beings and the fact that sometimes we have to oppose wrong and even evil behavior, compliance with a simple command can be challenging. To love others is not an easy quest, and is not meant to be. We have to lean on God for understanding and strength, constantly reexamining our thoughts and actions toward others. Since becoming a Christian, I have tried to keep that purpose before me in all endeavors, to love God and

---

[4] Mark 12:29-30.

others to the best of my ability and, by doing so, to contribute something to God's kingdom. I believe that there is a higher authority, a higher loyalty, and a higher purpose of this nature calling each of us.

Many fortunate young people have an understanding already of what it means to live purpose-driven Christian lives. Your challenge will be to hold onto your faith through the many trials that will come from an indifferent and even antagonistic culture.

For those who have rejected their spiritual heritage, or who actually have never had one, I strongly urge you to consider taking on the role of *seeker*—one who is continually and diligently seeking answers to life's hard questions. One of your first intellectual tasks as an adult should be to find out why you exist and for what purpose. God honors those who accept this task with an open heart and seeking mind. Read, study, pray, and ask questions. As a wise philosopher once said, "Large skepticism leads to large understanding. No skepticism leads to no understanding."

I will refrain from evangelizing at this point except to reiterate my belief that Jesus Christ is the answer to the fundamental questions of life about meaning and purpose. I have written *A Skeptic's Guide to God* to fully explain how and why this is true. For now, I urge you to simply consider the importance of *belief* in something. It seems that more and more teachers and professors are discouraging belief in anything. A scientific paper I recently read made this assertion: "Belief is the curse of the thinking class," placing *doubt* on a higher moral plane than *belief*. I followed this path of thought for a long time, and I found it led to a meaningless world in which my own efforts appeared to be meaningless as well. You have to believe in something to lead a purpose-driven life.

So, now we come back to applying the principles of war to daily life, keeping in mind this perspective of a higher loyalty and ultimate purpose. *Principles* for living come to life only with a clear understanding of your *purpose* for living.

> *"Teacher, which is the greatest commandment in the Law?" Jesus replied: "'Love the Lord your God with all your heart and with all your soul and with all your mind. This is the first and greatest commandment. And the second is like it: 'Love your neighbor as yourself .:All the Law and the Prophets hang on these two commandments."* **Matthew 22:36-40**

> *Dear friends, since God so loved us, we also ought to love one another . . . if we love one another, God lives in us and his love is made complete in us.* **1 John 4:11-12**

> *That is why we labor and strive, because we have put our hope in the living God, who is the Savior of all people.* **1 Timothy 4:10**

Like arrows in the hands of a warrior are children born in one's youth.[5]

A Special Note

Lani Hillwig Spivey was my wife for forty-seven years on earth, and my love forevermore. She was an amazing woman who, among her many attributes, was a perfect Marine wife. When asked by a Marine general why I had not been to Happy Hour at the Officers' Club for some time, she famously replied, "Well General, I take care of *happy hour* for Larkin all by myself." The subject was not mentioned again. I refer to Lani often in the pages to come, since most of the lessons I share come from our life together and the wisdom we hopefully gained together. I have highlighted her specific advice for young women in Appendix B.

I am thankful for my children, **Anastasia, Bayliss, Catherine Alexa, and Windom**, who have helped me write this book by sharing some of their recollections and lessons learned growing up in a family

---

[5] Psalm 127:4

with an overly conservative father and a boundlessly joyful mother.

This book is dedicated to **Sophie Wenz**, my oldest grandchild. She is the first of my descendants to undertake active military service, of which I am extremely proud and somewhat fearful. She, however, is not fearful and will be an amazing Soldier. As our oldest grandchild, she has set the bar of care and kindness for her siblings and cousins, creating a climate of love, unity, and comradery within our extended family that would not have existed without her.

To all of my grandchildren: **Sophie, Owen, Charlotte, Anabelle, Larkin, Radik, Calder, Cousteau, Kepler, and Rosalie**. I have written this book with you at the forefront of my thoughts. I know you miss your Nani, as do I, and I regret that you do not have her physically present to shower you with the love, admiration, encouragement, and advice that she had for each of you. I have tried to preserve some of her in this book, which I know is a poor substitute. Just know that she and I love each of you deeply and follow your progress in life closely.

You will grieve, but your grief will turn into joy. **John 16:20**

Git there firstest with the mostest![6]

Chapter One

Mass

MASS for Warriors: **To concentrate the effects of combat power at the place and time to achieve decisive results.**[7] Vital to the concept of mass is having the insight to identify the decisive place and time in which to attack the enemy's critical vulnerability. We seek mass to overwhelm the enemy in an attempt to deliver the decisive blow.[8]

---

[6] Colorful adaptation of a quote by Gen. Nathan Bedford Forrest, Army of the Confederacy, summarizing several principles of war, including Mass.

[7] The Joint Staff Officer's Guide 2000, JFSC Pub 1, Joint Forces Staff College, U. S. Government Printing Office, Washington, D.C., Appendix D-1.

[8] Tactical Fundamentals, B2B2269, U.S.M.C. Basic School, Quantico, Virginia, p. 7.

The first time I consciously applied the principle of Mass was during the tactical nuclear exercise at Command and Staff College. As the attacking force, we had at our disposal a ten kiloton nuclear device (for exercise purposes only), delivered by artillery. The defenders had a similar weapon, which can basically obliterate one grid square, or a one thousand by one thousand meter area. The problem for the attacker was to mass sufficient forces to decisively defeat the defender, without presenting a target for his nuclear weapon. So, from our perspective, the exercise was about how, when, and where to focus forces for the main attack. The tension felt during this process was intense. Ultimately, we were the losers in this battle when our "enemy" deduced our plan and obliterated our main maneuver element and our headquarters. We were outdone in applying the first principle of war.

To consider how this principle relates to more peaceful pursuits, I would equate the principle of mass in war to the idea of focus in life. I have already revealed my belief that God must be our ultimate focus, but this does not mean that we are all to be priests or missionaries. Most of us have talents and interests that rightly lead into a myriad of directions, including every conceivable occupation and profession. Life in the modern world truly offers an unlimited array of choices. Successful men and women in every career field have roles to play in serving God that is equally and, at times, even more important than that of any priest or missionary.

When Lani and I were doing college visits with one of our children, we had an interesting discussion with an admissions officer at one of our prospective schools. Besides test scores and essays, he, like other admissions officers, was very interested in the applicant's high school and community activities. He stated that he was not as impressed, however, with the variety of their involvements and accomplishments as he was with the depth of commitment to a few or even one activity. His comments exemplified the application of the principle of Mass and the importance of focus at this and every stage of life.

For some young people, professional focus comes early and easily. If this is you, you know already you want to be a doctor or fireman and go about your academic years with a singular pursuit in mind. I've always considered such individuals fortunate, since my own experience was so different. Like most of my contemporaries, I chose a major in college arbitrarily, and then did my first year in military service more or less fulfilling a family tradition. By age twenty-three, however, I faced the need to make a decision about my professional life. After reaching the frustrating realization that God was not going to tell me what to do, I made a long and thorough inventory of my talents and interests, coming to the conclusion that a career in the Marine

Corps was my "calling." From that point, my focus was indeed intense.

At that point, I was also unmarried with no obligations other than those to the Corps. I could afford to volunteer for every school or assignment, with no regard about separation from family or danger to myself. I considered myself highly focused and on the "fast track" for many years. Later on, as I had to integrate other priorities into my life, I would learn that there are times when being overly focused on one thing can run amok. I will explain in coming chapters the other principles of war pertaining to this phenomenon.

For now, we will look at the effort required in our chosen careers or professions to emphasize the main point of Mass: Success in any and every area of professional life does not come easily and requires focus, at times intense focus. You will have to concentrate your physical, emotional, and intellectual energies to learn and advance. Always take inventory of what you do and don't know, striving to expand your knowledge and expertise. Keep track of your competition. Volunteer for anything that significantly adds to your experience, even the menial tasks. Come in early and stay late. Be on time—don't waste others' time. Strive to understand and master the job of your boss. Make yourself indispensable.

MASS for Millennials—FOCUS your efforts.

> *Whatever you do, work at it with all your heart, as working for the Lord, not for men.* **Colossians 3:23**

> *Fire will test the quality of each man's work. If what he has built survives, he will receive his reward.* **1 Corinthians 3:13-14**

"Having lost sight of what we are trying to accomplish, we need to re-double our efforts!"[9]

Chapter Two

Objective

OBJECTIVE for Warriors: **To direct every military operation toward a clearly defined, decisive, and attainable objective.** Related to mass and economy of force, we must know where to mass and where to economize, which is defined by a decisive objective.[10]

In combat, commanders accomplish their assigned missions by breaking the overall task down into specific and attainable objectives for subordinate units. Every night, as a company commander, I assigned each of my platoon commanders an area to defend and avenues of approach to cover. They, in turn, gave their men specific

---

[9] Ironic exhortation of an old corps gunnery sergeant.

[10] Same sources cited in Chapter One,

sectors of fire and positions to defend. On the move, I was given an axis (direction) of advance with intermediate and final objectives, and gave similar guidance to my platoons. The military approach summarized in this principle is to give clear objectives, accompanied by the widest possible latitude in attaining them.

This is a good approach to managing any organization, and even your personal and family life. Overall goals are best attained by focusing on specific things that need to be accomplished. A lot of prioritizing is of course in order. Some tasks are more important than others, and some things are not worth completing at all.

In applying this principle to daily living, the idea of balance is important. In 2008, my wife, Lani, and her sister were with their father in the hospital near the end of his life. One morning the doctor came into the room, at which time Lani's dad introduced her sister as "my Phi Beta Kappa daughter." After a pause, understanding she was about to be ignored, Lani offered, "I was good on the balance beam!" The doctor looked at her, smiled, and said, "Well, in life, balance is everything." In retelling this story on herself, Lani incorporated the doctor's statement as one of her important mottoes: *Balance in life is everything.* It should be a motto for each of us.

Under the principle of Mass, I emphasized focus. For most of my college and professional life, I felt an intense pressure to prove myself. I don't think this is uncommon for most people, especially young adults. In any new job, this pressure can be all consuming. Sooner or later, however, we have to face the fact that there are things perhaps even more important than professional or monetary success. This is especially true when others become involved in our lives. When we have a family, a single-minded focus on work can run rampant.

This is where the subject of balance comes into play. I have learned that for me, there are four vital, interrelated areas that need to be balanced constantly. These are **spiritual, family, professional, and physical health**. Each requires periodic reassessment, focus, and well-thought-out objectives.

You know where I stand on the importance of your **spiritual** life. Whether believer or seeker, you should put the pursuit of spiritual understanding and growth high on your priority list. This can be considered, "Making the main thing the main thing." Believers need to have a plan to pray, study, and do the work they are meant to do for God's kingdom. Some of these activities require special time and attention, like prayer and Bible study. However, you will also need to incorporate these activities into your daily life at home and work in a conscious manner, with clearly defined objectives. Pray before classes, meetings, and interviews. Praise and encourage others publicly, while criticizing or disciplining privately. Always stress the positive whenever possible. Work references to God into your conversations and even share your own witness when appropriate. Non-believers should continue conscientiously seeking answers to their doubts and questions. Read, study, think, question. There are actually "seeker" churches waiting to encourage you on this path. I strongly suggest you not drift along in the spiritual area of your life.

In our **family** lives, most of us go about our daily routines hoping we are doing okay as spouses, parents, and/or as children. And we do accomplish a lot by just "being there" in these roles. Those without a parent or spouse can attest to this fact. However, these roles in life also call for intentional focus and objectives of their own. I believe that only God comes before your family in importance, and God himself is pleased when you put your family first before other worldly concerns. You do this not only in the everyday love and affection you show family members, but also by planning specific activities, by doing acts of service, by giving recognition for accomplishments, and a myriad of other initiatives. All of these deserve intentional planning on your part.

I won't say too much about **professional** objectives, since this was the focus of the discussion on focus itself in chapter one (Mass). Career goals are a good thing and you will need intermediate objectives along the way to accomplish them. But for now, we're talking about balance. You probably know successful men and women who have sacrificed everything to get where they are. You may choose to do the same, and there may even be times when you have no choice. But never lose sight of the fact that this area of your life, even though extremely important, is ultimately meaningless if your relationships with God and your family are broken. Never stop asking yourself, "What am I working for?"

It's also hard to accomplish much in any area of life if your **physical health** is not what it should be. I once attended a Marine Corps seminar on physical fitness, chaired by Dr. Kenneth Cooper, the father of what was then called *aerobics*. I have always remembered his statement, "If you can't find two hours in your week (basically 20 minutes per day) to devote to your physical fitness, your priorities in life are out of order." This statement was extreme underkill for Marines, but it has nevertheless stuck with me ever since. Good health is easy for a young person to take for granted. However, young people, take it from a much older person, time spent focusing on this area while young is like putting money in the bank for later, when good health definitely can't be taken for granted. You will also find that staying in good physical condition adds to your quality of life at every age.

The military idea of objective is simple: You get better results from those under your command if you spell out your mission in clearly attainable accomplishments. This approach is especially useful for ordering your own activities and motivating yourself to success. A difficult assignment can always be broken down into smaller parts. Get started! Do the easy things first. Take one step at a time. And remember, *balance* in life is everything.

OBJECTIVE for Millennials—Have **GOALS.** Maintain **BALANCE** in your life.

> *Do you not know that in a race all runners run, but only one gets the prize? Run in such a way to get the prize. Everyone who competes in the games goes into strict training. They do it to get a crown that will not last; but we do it to get a crown that will last forever.* **1 Corinthians 9:24-25**

Retreat Hell! We're attacking in a new direction.[11]

Chapter Three

Offensive

OFFENSIVE for Warriors: **To seize, retain, and exploit the initiative.** Maintaining an offensive mindset does not imply that we seek to avoid defense. Rather it implies the use of the defense as a temporary expedient to prepare to resume the offense. Offense being the decisive form of combat, it is the method by which we exploit the enemy vulnerability, impose our will, and determine the course of the war.[12]

The quote at the top of this page came from the Commanding General of the First Marine Division during the Korean War. His division was extended far into North Korea, near the Chosen Reservoir, when China suddenly came into the war, threatening

---

[11] Gen. O.P. Smith, USMC, leading the First Marine Division in the epic Chosen Reservoir campaign, Korea, 1950.

[12] Same sources cited in Chapter One.

to surround and cut off the Marines. General Smith refused to characterize the battle that followed as a withdrawal, instead rightfully telling the world and his men that they were "attacking in a new direction." There are times in life when we can all use this mindset. If you get a bad grade, fail a course, or even get fired from a job, this is not the time to sulk or become defensive. Consider what you do next as attacking in a new direction. Maintain an offensive mindset.

The principle of offensive also stresses the importance of action or doing something, even in the absence of complete information. Marines consider this an important attitude in combat. A positive course of action proves more effective than delay in a tense and confusing situation. The default position for Marines is almost always: *Take the initiative.*

Dick Camp, a fellow company commander in Vietnam, described an action near Con Tien when his unit was attacked by a large North Vietnamese Army force. As his men encountered incoming hand grenades, they realized that enemy troops had penetrated to within a few feet of their lines in dense undergrowth. Sergeant Marshall Jesperson, a squad leader in Third Platoon, decided it was up to him to deal with this threat. He quickly passed the word to his squad and got them ready. On his order, they stood up and assaulted into the thicket. There was a crescendo of small arms fire, accompanied by shouts and the sounds of close in-fighting with bayonets and knives. The fight was swift and brutal, as the Marines cleared out the threat to their lines. Camp later thought about the actions of his squad leader and the young Marines under him: "Jesperson realized what had to be done, and he did it. No one told him to lead the way into the thicket . . . He did what he did because it had to be done. More important, those eighteen- and nineteen-year-old Marines followed him. They could have stayed in their fighting holes. No one held a roll call." One young leader's initiative and swift, offensive action saved the day for his beleaguered unit.

If you can show some kind of initiative on the job or in any group activity, you will clearly separate your-self from the pack. You will almost always find plenty of people around you who are vocal in their com-plaints and generous with advice—but short on action. If you step up and take the lead in solving a problem, big or small, you will stand out. Often it's a matter of thinking enough about your situation to actually *see* that a problem exists. Such employees or team members with this initiative are few and far between.

The idea of offensive action also goes hand in hand with a general positive attitude. My father once gave me advice, as I was trying to prepare a baccalau-reate speech for my high school graduation. He sug-gested a simple theme: "Let the older people provide the wisdom and guidance. The young people (those of us graduating) need to provide the world with energy and optimism." I think this is still good advice today. Enthusiasm is a particular quality of youth and should be put to good use. We don't accomplish much by looking back or being defensive, and not too many pessimists are pleasant to be around. Lani kept a ruler in our kitchen inscribed with words motivating her to climb Mt. Kilimanjaro: "*If you can DREAM it . . . you can ACHIEVE it.*" She always epitomized this kind of positive attitude in her life.

I also remembering hearing my uncle, Collins Spivey, give some excellent advice on this subject. Someone was complaining to him about how bad the world situation seemed to be. He responded back with, "Times have always seemed bad!" citing events during his lifetime such as the Great Depression and the dire days of World War II. He said that life goes on even in bad times, and you have to have faith that the bad things will come to an end. His advice was to live your life optimistically. Never let your worries get you down. Always expect and plan for a better future.

Unfortunately, there are times in our lives when a cheerful attitude is hard to find. Tragedies await each of us and are inevitable parts of life. One thing I have learned, however, and this from fellow veterans who survived many hard times in combat: When a tragic event brings you closer to God, there can always be a positive outcome. What happens to us is not nearly as important as what we do as a result of the experience. We respond positively when we turn to God, seek His comfort, and attempt to discern His perspective on time and the events which have hurt us. Our attitude is truly the one thing that we have complete control over in our lives. With a positive attitude, I have seen many use their own tragic experiences as a platform to help others in similar circumstances. Many have found their life's purpose in tragedy.

In one sense, Jesus's ministry on earth can be seen as the ultimate victory of the offensive over the defensive mindset. Most religions have traditionally placed burdens on their followers to live up to rules and regulations, and to please God by following the letter of some set of laws. Jesus promised instead to "put my laws in their minds and write them on their hearts."[13] And as the apostle Paul said, "God demonstrates his own love for us in this: While we were still sinners, Christ died for us."[14] So, through faith in Jesus, we know that we are loved by God, forgiven of our wrongdoings, and freed to live positively and joyfully in His service.

OFFENSIVE for Millennials — Be POSITIVE.

If you hold to my teaching, you are really my disciples. Then you will know the truth and the truth will set you free. So if the Son sets you free, you will be free indeed. **John 8:32, 36**

---

[13] Hebrews 8:10

[14] Romans 5:8

If the enemy is in range, so are you.[15]

Chapter Four

Security

SECURITY for Warriors: **To never permit the enemy to acquire unexpected advantage.** We look to adopt measures to prevent the enemy from imposing their will on us faster than we can react. It does not imply the over-application of caution to eliminate risk, but rather seeks to enhance our operations through bold maneuver and acceptance of calculated risk.[16]

While commanding a Marine rifle company in combat, I tried to eliminate every risk that I could think of, calculated or otherwise. On the move, we put out point guards, rear guards, and flank security. If possible, we had air support on station and artillery support on call and pre-planned. We avoided well-used trails and made sure the

---

[15] Wisdom from the Old Corps.

[16] Same sources cited in Chapter One.

troops were dispersed at all times. Noise and camouflage discipline were strictly enforced. We stayed off the skyline. At night, listening posts and ambushes went out, and fire support was planned and often rehearsed. Fifty percent alert was common, even though an extreme burden on exhausted troops. These precautions were never perfect or foolproof, but were religiously looked to every hour of every day by every small unit leader.

Later in my career, I was the designated Disaster Preparedness Officer for a Marine Corps base in California. It was my job to coordinate planning for every contingency, including mobilizing for general war, coping with nuclear, biological, and chemical attack, and recovering from natural and manmade disasters. I also had to marshal the resources to implement those plans. Over the years, I applied much of the same mindset to my family life, trying to anticipate and, where possible, eliminate risk. Lani went along with this by and large, lovingly calling me her own "disaster preparedness officer."

Our primary focus, like that of any young person or family, was financial security, which was a difficult state to obtain in a military family. One of my fellow officers once commented that we lived a life of "genteel poverty." Our family was better off than most, but we still had to work hard to balance our budget, a challenge at any income level. So far as contingency planning, we had to rely on life insurance and a savings account built up doggedly. In that regard, we always tried to make sure we lived one pay grade below where we actually were, banking the difference. Lani fully supported this plan, which would have gone nowhere otherwise. This gave us a pretty good nest egg when the time came to buy our first home in Charleston, South Carolina.

Every person and every family has to make a tradeoff between nest egg building and consumption or, as it's said in the military, between "guns and butter." If you are on your own, this tradeoff is up to you. As a married couple, Lani and I guarded each of these areas respectively; I the guns and she the butter. We came together most of the time and achieved a pretty good balance. I often relented for the sake of family morale, as she did for the sake of family security. Except for our home and, occasionally our car, we stayed out of debt.

Financial security is, of course, only part of the picture. For many years my family has lived in a hurricane zone with all the intendent risks of isolation, flooding, and loss of power. Wherever you live, it is very unlikely you will be immune to some form of natural or manmade disruption. It is my firm belief that every family everywhere should be able to sustain itself for at least a week. One of the most pathetic things I've seen is a woman interviewed in the aftermath of Hurricane Katrina, complaining, "It's been three days and no one has come to help us!" We see frequent disasters that overwhelm the relief agencies, so thinking people of all ages should plan accordingly.

Real "preppers" look at the possibility of more extended disasters, such as loss of the power grid, financial meltdown, or breakdown of law and order. They plan and prepare for such eventualities by trying to achieve total self-sufficiency. Although most of us are not so inclined or dedicated, we all could use a little of the prepper mentality. Modern freeze-dried food with long shelf lives makes food storage more feasible. Water purification means are available if considered before the emergency. Some amount of gold, silver, ammunition and other critical supplies can be accumulated, as the budget permits, for a day when these might come in handy and be difficult to acquire.

Due to my military background, I have always been comfortable with firearms and have maintained a concealed weapons permit and proficiency on the range. Lani bought into this herself and passed the CWP course, shooting the center out of her first target. If this is foreign to you, you might consider visiting a local gun shop. Plenty of help is available to familiarize you with various firearms and help you get into shooting. Young women especially need to seriously consider this form of self-defense.

As a teenager, I had an amateur radio license and used my small transmitter to contact others around the world on voice and code. More recently, in consideration of my prepper tendencies, I have reinstated that license to give the family a means of internal communication and solar-sustained contact with the outside world. In the present age of cell phones and internet, this may strike you as pretty far-fetched. I sincerely hope you are right.

The desire for security is powerful and obvious to most. Maybe it's a function of age that we become more and more conscious of the threat of economic, natural, environmental, and health-related disasters. Sometimes these threats are real, and sometimes they are overblown, but in all cases they are exploited by sensation-seeking media. At this point, it is well to go back to the military definition of Security stated above and emphasize the point that we should not be paralyzed by our concern for safety. We should each do our best to be prepared for likely events, at the same time recognizing that we will never be prepared for everything. Also, I have learned over the years that most situations do turn out better than my dark thoughts anticipate, and that I should be more optimistic about the future generally. Finally, we each must realize that our ultimate security lies in something beyond our bank accounts, life insurance, food storage, police protection, and government in general. Ultimately, our security lies in the strength of character, purpose, and peace of mind that we can find only in God.

During the darkest days of World War II, when Germany seemed victorious over most of Europe, the king of England shared a poignant message with the free people of the world. Quoting from a favorite poem, he stated,

> *I said to the man who stood at the Gate of the Year, "Give me a light that I may tread safely into the unknown." And he replied, "Go out into the darkness and put your hand into the Hand of*

God. That shall be to you better than light, and safer than a known way."[17]

SECURITY for Millennials—Be **PREPARED**.

For you were once in darkness, but now you are light in the Lord. Live as children of light (for the fruit of the light consists in all goodness, righteousness and truth) and find out what pleases the Lord. **Ephesians 5:8-10**

The Lord will watch over your coming and going both now and forevermore. **Psalm 121:8**

---

[17] King George VI 1939 Christmas day broadcast, www.royaloak. gov.uk. The poem was written by Minnie Louise Haskins in 1908 and was a favorite of Queen Elizabeth.

*Never send a man where you can send a bullet
(or a thousand pound bomb).*[18]

Chapter Five

Economy of Force

ECONOMY OF FORCE for Warriors: **To allocate minimum essential combat power at the place and time to achieve decisive results.** This goes hand in hand with the concept of Mass. In order to concentrate decisive combat power at the decisive point, we must know where to economize forces at our secondary efforts. This also implies an acceptance of calculated risk at these secondary efforts.[19]

I once heard one of my "veterans" in Vietnam explain to a brand new guy, known affectionately as a BNG, "Don't ever run when you can walk; don't stand up when you can sit down; and don't do anything when

---

[18] Wisdom from grunts of the Old Corps.

[19] Same sources cited in Chapter One.

you can sleep!" He was explaining, as only a Marine can, the principle of Economy of Force. Troop leaders apply this principle in combat by not needlessly expending the energy of the men under them. Before commanders start planning and strategizing their next moves, they ensure the troop's needs are taken care of, not the least of which are rest and relaxation. Trust has to be built within combat units that the leaders are doing their best to tend to the needs of their troops *before* those times when they have to demand superhuman effort.

The principle applies on the drill field as well. There military men and women learn the discipline of listening to and executing orders in a precise way. If a unit is called to "attention," the proper position is taken and maintained. If "at ease" is given, everyone can relax. A good drill instructor would not keep his unit at attention for one moment longer than necessary. If being at attention for a prolonged period is required in a ceremony or parade, everyone involved understands the reason why.

Needless expenditure of energy is an issue for all of us, young and old. I have been my own worst enemy in this. Too often, I find myself committed to unimportant or ineffective activity at the expense of the important things that matter, as already discussed: spiritual, family, professional, and physical health. I know I *should* be doing better, but as the apostle Paul said, "What I want to do I do not do, but what I hate I do."[20] Our motives can get complicated, but, consid-

---

[20] Romans 7:15.

ering health as an important concern, each of us needs to incorporate some downtime in our lives to stay mentally and physically healthy. Again, balance in life is everything!

In my case, the biggest and clearest drain on my energy has always been anxiety. Before I became a Christian, this problem was acute. I worried about almost everything and, often, was not even sure exactly what I was worried about. I've already mentioned my role in life as a disaster preparedness officer. My mantra was, "Hope for the best, plan for the worst." Well, hope is ephemeral, but the planning is highly focused and specific. So the focus was on the bad things that could happen more so than the hope part. This is a great outlook for a prepper, but not so much for a general human being and family member, where a degree of confidence and optimism about the future is appreciated by all.

It seems that problems associated with depression keep growing among young people as well. Alarmingly, I see and hear about more apathy, depression, and even suicide among teenagers and young adults, the very people who should be primed with energy and enthusiasm. I can only speculate on the causes. Social media seems to paint a rosier picture of other people's lives than our own, while also providing a platform for bullying and demeaning from a distance. Our movies and music glorify sex and violence, and even depression itself. I believe these are spiritual assaults on our well-being and that the only sure defense against them is in the spiritual dimension.

I was lifted from my own mire of pessimism by Jesus Christ. I mention this fact now mainly for the benefit of readers who consider themselves seekers. When my search brought me to Jesus (at age fifty-three), I seriously considered for the first time His words: "Who of you by worrying can add a single hour to his life? Do not worry about tomorrow, for tomorrow will worry about itself."[21] Almost from the moment I accepted Jesus as Lord, those ill-defined anxieties that I described in me disappeared, and my actual problems took on a different focus. I was able to at least consider God's perspective on my troubles, finding the confidence that most things actually do work out for the best. I also acquired the firm conviction that if any problem caused me to reach out to God and come closer to Him, then there was no problem that couldn't have a good outcome. I have been forced to put this belief to the test, and I can bear witness that it holds true in bad times. Most of my brothers and sisters in Christ have the same witness to share.

As mentioned, my faith has relieved my anxieties to a large extent. However, at times I still drift back toward my old habits. I now consider my level of worry a pretty good barometer of where I stand with my faith. There are times when I have to refocus and reenergize spiritually. Most believers can identify with this need.

---

[21] Matthew 6:27, 34.

In general, however, those with faith are able to tap into a great economy of force in life by applying their faith to their daily problems and by lifting their worries to the one with the true solutions. Then, they are able to focus their efforts on the problems they can actually solve and the good works they can accomplish.

ECONOMY OF FORCE for Millennials — WORRY less, **DO** more.

> *There is a time for everything, and a season for every activity under heaven: a time to be born and a time to die . . . a time to tear down and a time to build . . . a time to weep and a time to laugh . . . a time to be silent and a time to speak.* **Ecclesiastes 3:1-4, 7**

If your attack is going really well, you're probably walking into an ambush.[22]

Chapter Six

Maneuver

MANEUVER for Warriors: To place the enemy in a position of disadvantage through the flexible application of combat power. The essence of maneuver is taking action to generate and exploit some kind of advantage over the enemy, as a means of accomplishing our objectives as effectively as possible. That advantage may be psychological, technological, or temporal as well as spatial. Especially important is maneuver in time.[23]

The principle of Maneuver follows and amplifies the principle of Offensive. Winning the battle usually

---

[22] Wisdom of the Old Corps.

[23] Same sources cited in Chapter One.

31

requires some form of planned, dynamic movement. There is an Old Corps proverb that applies: "Anything you do can get you shot, including nothing." The old gunnery sergeant would add: "*Especially* nothing!" As previously stated, the default position for Marines and soldiers in combat is to take the initiative and "move out."

General Douglas MacArthur's attack on Inchon during the Korean War is the classic example of maneuver in war. With the North Korean invasion stopped and contained along the Pusan perimeter in the extreme southeastern corner of Korea, MacArthur sent the First Marine Division far behind the enemy's lines to land amphibiously at Inchon and strike directly at Seoul. This classic flanking maneuver precipitated the complete rout of North Korean forces engaged along the perimeter to the south.

Considering life as movement is a pretty good mindset for anyone, especially a young person. When I was a new Christian having trouble deciding what kind of church work I should be doing, a friend said to me, "Well Larkin, God can't steer a parked car!" In other words, you have to be moving before God can help you adjust your course. This advice can be useful for anyone facing uncertainty in his or her life. Sometimes we wait too long for just the right course of action, when we could be making progress by doing the worthwhile tasks right in front of us. C.S. Lewis touched on this point in his book *Screwtape Letters,* when the senior devil exhorts his subordinate: "Keep his (the person he is trying to win for satan) mind off the most elementary duties by directing it to the most advanced and spiritual ones."[24] Satan is happy when we stymie ourselves into inaction. So, do the menial tasks if they can get you started. Learn and grow as you go. Depending on your spiritual point of view, either you or God can adjust your course better if you are moving in some direction.

This advice is particularly useful in pursuit of spiritual understanding. Again, I express my sincere hope that if you do not have a relationship with God, you consider yourself a seeker. For you, the point is especially relevant: "God can't steer a parked car!" We have specific, biblical caution for anyone who is self-satisfied in his or her own knowledge: "And just as they did not see fit to acknowledge God any longer, God gave them over to a depraved mind, to do those things which are not proper."[25] To me, this is one of the most foreboding passages in the Bible, informing us that at some point, God might "give us over" to our own worldly and shallow thought processes. So, never get too comfortable in your own understanding. Be skeptical if you must, but don't be a parked car.

The concept of maneuver works especially well for believers. I have heard the Christian life best described as a *journey.* Some talk about their walk with Christ.

---

[24] C. S. Lewis, *Screwtape Letters.* New York: MacMillan Paperbacks Edition, 1960. , p. 25.

[25] Romans 1:28, New American Standard Bible.

What you should picture is *movement*, for you are going somewhere. You are directing your path toward God. You want to know Him, and you want to please Him. You can do both to a degree, but in this lifetime, you are probably not going to do either completely. You will have a sense of direction, but you will not likely reach a final destination. There will always be new horizons ahead. Some parts of the journey will be smooth and effortless, while others will be difficult. Sometimes God will seem close, while sometimes He will seem far away. You will undoubtedly need help as you travel. God's promise to you is that He will be with you. Your efforts and His grace will bring you ever closer.

Sometimes this kind of positive movement in our lives is hampered by fear of the unknown. In Vietnam, one of the airbases had an enemy sniper who fired on aircraft landing and taking off. Amazingly, the sniper never hit anything. When the base commander started sending out patrols to eliminate the threat, the airmen exhorted him to leave the sniper alone, fearing he might be replaced by someone who could actually shoot! In *Hamlet,* William Shakespeare gave us the famous phrase explaining how our fear, "makes us rather bear the ills we have than fly to others that we know not of." We all prefer the familiar to the unknown. To combat this kind of fear, periodically move out of one of your comfort zones. Take the risks that come with moving toward new relationships and new perspectives.

MANEUVER for Millennials—Don't sit still. Keep **MOVING** ahead.

Be strong and courageous. Do not be terrified; do not be discouraged, for the Lord your God will be with you wherever you go. **Joshua 1:9**

Either lead, follow, or get out of the way![26]

Chapter Seven

Unity of Command

UNITY OF COMMAND for Warriors: **To ensure unity of effort under one responsible commander for every objective.** Mass, economy of force, and maneuver would be impossible without the vision of a single leader. To ensure the vision is carried to the lowest levels, while still allowing for flexibility and initiative, we use commander's intent.[27]

Unity of Command under one leader presupposes a certain degree of good leadership that is fair, firm, and respected. In the American military establishment of today, the leadership model of "rank has its privilege" has largely disappeared, replaced by the model

---

[26] Exhortation of a frustrated soldier trying to take charge in a chaotic situation.

[27] Same sources cited in Chapter One.

of servant leadership. In other words, the interests of subordinates come before those of the leader himself. Under this model, leaders build trust over time before they have to give difficult orders to accomplish dangerous missions. In the Marine Corps, this approach was exemplified by the renowned Chesty Puller who, as a regimental commander, would often be seen standing in chow lines with his men, excoriating junior officers for cutting into the line.

My first piece of advice on leadership came from my father, who said to me while I was a Citadel cadet, "It says in the Bible, 'If you would be first among them, you must be servant to all.'" Later in life, I learned that these were in fact the words of Jesus Christ, as found in Matthew 20:26-28. Jesus Himself originated and exemplified the concept of servant leadership: "Your attitude should be the same as that of Christ Jesus: Who being in very nature God, did not consider equality with God something to be grasped, but made himself nothing, taking the very nature of a servant, being made in human likeness."[28] Taking the role of servant is not only the Christian thing to do, it is the only way to gain the respect of those you seek to lead.

The definition of Unity of Command above mentions the idea of "commander's intent." Military operation orders always clearly spell out the commander's goal, or his vision for ultimate success. Although detailed orders and objectives are then given to subordinate

---

[28] Philippians 2: 5-7.

units, the commander's intent gives every member of the command the knowledge required to persevere in the confusion of combat and to take individual initiative, if required. This concept can be useful to each of us in many situations. When we make the effort to share the big picture with troops, family members, team members, or employees, we make them part of a team with a clear understanding of what we're all trying to accomplish.

To give a Ranger School example of this idea, on my last patrol I was called up to the head of the column at about 2 am and told that I was to take over as the patrol *leader*. I swallowed hard and proceeded to gather everyone around. I went over our planned raid at dawn and reiterated one of our missions: to recover a vital missile component. The next morning, during the confusion of our attack, one of my fellow Rangers came to me with the missile component, having found it while clearing one of the buildings. By knowing the big picture and taking the initiative, he enabled us to complete our mission ahead of schedule and to clear the area before the expected counter attack.

When it comes to unity of command in the family, we face a more controversial topic in the present age of women's rights. Biblically, we have the injunction, "Wives, submit to your husbands as to the Lord,"[29] which does not sit well with many modern women. I find it helpful, however, to put this passage in perspective by

---

[29] Ephesians 5:22.

looking at the Scripture surrounding it. In the preceding verse, we read, "Submit to one another out of reverence for Christ," and following, "Husbands, love your wives, just as Christ loved the church and gave himself for her." Someone may have to submit to someone on some occasion, but a loving couple should be able to reach consensus most of the time. Being a good Christian woman, Lani gave me the tie-breaker, although I did not use it often. I asked her to submit to me on one important occasion against her wishes when I decided we should stay in the Marine Corps. One of the most touching moments of my life came when I found a note she wrote before her death thanking me for making that decision.

In any relationship, submitting to others when possible and appropriate is necessary. However, of even greater importance is the need for a higher authority. Christians can turn to the Bible and Jesus, where God's wisdom can be found to answer many of the questions and disputes we face today. As a couple, or any group of people, strives to come ever closer to God, they come closer to each other in the process. Lani and I did our best to apply this idea to our marriage. Seeing ourselves as the base of a triangle, we viewed Jesus at the pinnacle. Our marriage was blessed as we moved upward toward the pinnacle and ever closer to each other.

UNITY OF COMMAND for Millennials—Be a
SERVANT leader. Seek a **HIGHER** authority.

> *Whoever wants to become great among you
> must be your servant, and whoever wants to
> be first must by your slave— just as the Son
> of Man did not come to be served, but to serve,
> and to give his life as a ransom for many.*
> **Matthew 20:26-28**

No plan survives first contact with the enemy.[30]

Chapter Eight

Surprise

SURPRISE for Warriors: **To strike the enemy at a time or place or in a manner for which it is unprepared.** It does not require the enemy to be caught unaware, but rather that he becomes aware too late to react effectively. May include the use of speed, unexpected forces, operating at night, deception, security, variation in techniques, and use of unfavorable terrain.[31]

For several months I commanded a reconnaissance unit in the vicinity of Hue, the ancient capital of Vietnam. Our mission was to patrol the mountains to the west of the city to discover and interdict enemy activity. These patrols were small, squad size

---

[30] An ancient and first principle of war.

[31] Same sources cited in Chapter One.

units operating deep in Viet Cong controlled territory. Stealth and surprise were the tools of our trade and our only guarantee of survival. We set ambushes, called in artillery and airstrikes, and planned our movements with extreme care. In all aspects, we paid careful attention to the principle of Surprise.

Later, in civilian life, one of my friends once planned a surprise vacation for himself and his wife. He secretly made the reservations, bought the plane tickets, made up an elaborate ruse about a routine business trip, and then popped the "surprise" just before boarding the aircraft. Lani listened to the telling of this story with great enthusiasm, but later turned to me and said emphatically, "Don't *ever* do that to me!" I could have guessed her reaction as we had already in our marriage disavowed the concept of surprise parties for birthdays, anniversaries, or other occasions.

In retrospect, I probably went along with this attitude a little too willingly, as it fit in so well with my conservative nature. In my high school yearbook I was voted "Most Dependable." This did not imply "most exciting." Lani always told me she felt secure in our marriage, probably reflecting what she perceived as my dependable nature. As explained in the chapter on Security, I was generally guardian of the budget and the one opposed to unplanned or frivolous (as I saw it) expenditures. In our ship of state, Lani always provided the sails, and I was supposed to be the rudder.

Frequently, however, I was the anchor, keeping us from going anywhere.

The lesson I draw from this family history is that it is well to consider a little more unpredictability in your life. This comes naturally to some, but unfortunately is a difficult concept for many in the introverts' camp. Those of us who are of a conservative, steady-as-she-goes nature should try occasionally to step out of that mold. This is one of my regrets in life, now that I no longer have that beautiful alter ego pulling me out of myself. I could have done so much more to make her life and that of my family more exciting, with more spontaneity in just about everything. Someone once said that no one has ever looked back on his life and wished he had *worked* harder. *Amen* to that.

Being less predictable has its application outside the family as well. Any quiet, self-contained person can benefit friends and fellow workers by stepping outside themselves occasionally. Be a little more spontaneous. Show enthusiasm over others' ideas and accomplishments. *Surprise* someone.

In the spiritual realm, I have found John Eldridge's approach to Christianity and life particularly inspiring. In his best-selling book, *Wild at Heart,* he explains that followers of Jesus don't need more rules, regulations, lists of things to do, or even *principles* to live by. Instead, he presents an exhalted picture of the Christian life as the greatest of all adventures, with battles to fight and risks to be taken. He shares the advice of a mentor: "Don't ask yourself what the world needs. Ask yourself what makes you come alive, and go do that, because what the world needs is people who have come alive."[32] With the freedom that we have in Jesus we are able to be much more than just *nice* people. We are able to do great things in his service, to surprise ourselves and others by living joyful, creative, and purpose-filled lives.

SURPRISE for Millennials—Be JOYFUL.

So I say, live by the Spirit . . . if you are led by the Spirit, you are not under law . . . the fruit of the Spirit is love, joy, peace, patience, kindness, goodness, faithfulness, gentleness and self-control. Against such things there is no law. **Galatians 5:16, 18, 22-23.**

---

[32] Eldridge, John. *Wild at Heart: Discovering the Secret of a Man's Soul*. Nashville, Tennessee: Nelson Books, 2001, *p.* 200.

Chapter Nine

Simplicity

SIMPLICITY for Warriors: **To prepare clear, uncomplicated and concise orders to ensure thorough understanding.** Plans and orders should be as simple and direct as the situation and mission dictate. This reduces the chance of misunderstandings that inject internal friction and, therefore, cause ineffective execution. Ceretus paribus (all variables being equal), the simplest plan is preferred.[34]

My First Sergeant advised me soon after I took command of Kilo Company, Third Battalion, Third Marines in Vietnam, "Captain, in the field, the simple things are the most important— however, they are usually the hardest to do." He was referring to such things as noise

---

[33] A universally recognized key to success.

[34] Same sources cited in Chapter One.

discipline, separation between men, camouflage, care of the feet, etc.—obvious, simple actions that would keep men alive and healthy. Still, in times of stress and fatigue, it took unrelenting effort and unbending discipline to ensure these things were done.

I had actually been introduced to the KISS formula before Vietnam, at Marine Basic School in Quantico, Virginia. As recent college graduates, we were introduced to the fact that young Marines function best with simple plans and specific orders. An attack with one clear objective and one moving part has a better chance of success than a complex scheme, no matter how ingenious. We, at first, laughingly derided this approach as, "Hey diddle diddle, right up the middle!"[35] After losing control of some of our own maneuver elements, however, most of us learned the value of such simplicity the hard way. The lesson was relearned every day in combat.

Simplicity is hard to find in our complex, everyday world. We immerse ourselves in work, family, church, charitable, and social activities, which fill our calendars and occupy our minds. Children multiply these concerns exponentially, making it often hard to focus on one thing at a time. The principles of Mass and Objective are especially relevant to this condition. To simplify your life, you sometimes have to rethink what you are involved in and eliminate some of the activities that you have voluntarily agreed to do. It also

---

[35] This expression has taken on a broader application, summarizing the "Marine way" of tackling problems in general.

helps to set clear goals, prioritize, do what can be done at the time, and then, cease worrying about what you haven't done.

In addition to these remedies, an important solution to life's confusion is available in the form of prayer. There is always something you can be thankful for in your life, and this should be your focus. When you thank God for your blessings, such as good health and a loving family, many complex worries fade away. You can share your problems with God, but first take inventory of your blessings and focus your prayers on the things for which you can be thankful.

My personal barrier to a spiritual life, up to the age of fifty-three, was my tendency to make all issues complicated. I studied comparative religions, pondered the difficult theological questions, and struggled to *self-actualize* myself. In college, I memorized William Butler Yeats's poem *Sailing to Byzantium*, which states in part:

> *O sages standing in God's holy fire As in the gold mosaic of a wall,*
> *Come from the holy fire, perne in a gyre, And be the singing-masters of my soul.*
> *Consume my heart away; sick with desire And fastened to a dying animal*
> *It knows not what it is; and gather me Into the artifice of eternity.*[36]

---

[36] Yeats, W. B. *Collected Poems*. New York: The Macmillan Company, 1956, p. 191.

My Citadel English professor and I spent a long time poring over the meaning of these complex words, which to me still defy interpretation or application to any useful action. But this was my intellectual life for decades, preferring complex riddles to simple truths.

My life changed when I finally faced the fact that, as a thinking human being, I could not ignore a very simple question: *Who is Jesus Christ?* And then I accepted the clear answer: *The Son of God, sent into the world to reconcile mankind to God.* With this simple acknowledgment, I took my first step of faith, which was not in any way a blind leap into the unknown; instead, it was accepting a simple and obvious truth, based on one of the most important and best documented events in history. KISS! Jesus is the Son of God.

In the Bible, we read how a worried father asked Jesus if He could do anything to help his sick son. Jesus said, "Everything is possible for him who believes." The father immediately exclaimed, "I do believe; help me overcome my unbelief!"[37] From my perspective, this story reveals God's plan for seekers and skeptical people like myself, and possibly you. Faith begins when you accept the simple truth: Jesus is who he says he is. From that point, God helps each of us in our unbelief by gradually resolving all the complex issues that occupy our minds and tend to keep us separated from Him.

---

[37] Mark 9:23-24.

SIMPLICITY for Millennials—Keep it **SIMPLE.**

I tell you the truth, unless you change and become like little children, you will never enter the kingdom of heaven. **Matthew 18:3**

Military power wins battles, but spiritual power wins wars.[38]

Summary

In the beginning, I conceded that applying the principles of war to daily life was probably a stretch. I'm sure readers will agree that I have stretched quite a bit. I have used (and perhaps abused) these principles as a framework for offering advice about daily living from a military perspective. I hope many young readers, especially my own grandchildren, find this advice useful. Once we come to an understanding of our purpose in life, we can simplify and apply the lessons of MOOSEMUSS as follows:

FOCUS your efforts.
(MASS)

Have **GOALS**. Maintain **BALANCE** in your life.
(OBJECTIVE)

---

[38] Gen. George C. Marshall.

Be **POSITIVE**.
(OFFENSIVE)

Be **PREPARED**.
(SECURITY)

WORRY less. **DO** more.
(ECONOMY OF FORCE)

Don't sit still. Keep **MOVING** ahead.
(MANEUVER)

Be a **SERVANT** leader. Seek a **HIGHER** authority.
(UNITY OF COMMAND)

Be **JOYFUL**.
(SURPRISE)

Keep it **SIMPLE**.
(SIMPLICITY)

Applying the Principles of War to life may seem on the surface to be somewhat *un-Christian*, and there may be some truth to that. I was not a Christian when I was a Marine, and my conscience never bothered me while learning about and applying military violence in defense of my nation. I remain confident in the belief that defense of myself, my loved ones, and my nation against evil is necessary and at times appropriate.

54

However, I appreciate that this is not a simple subject. Jesus commands us to *"turn the other cheek,"*[39] and I know that this admonition should apply in most situations. I think I know when it cannot be applied, but I try not to be too comfortable in my own understanding. In this book I have tried and hope that I have succeeded in presenting the Principles of War in a useful and practical way, not to fight with anyone, but to aid your journey toward a more positive and purposeful life.

> *Who shall separate us from the love of Christ? Shall trouble or hardship or persecution or famine or nakedness or danger or sword? No, in all these things we are more than conquerors through him who loved us. For I am convinced that neither death nor life, neither angels nor demons, neither the present nor the future, nor any powers, neither height nor depth, nor anything else in all creation will be able to separate us from the love of God that is in Christ Jesus our Lord.* **Romans 8:35, 37-39**

---

[39] Matthew 5:39

The easy way is always mined.[40]

Appendix A

Spiritual Warfare

So far, we have focused on the principles of war from our own perspective. However, it might be well to consider how they might also be used *against* us. There are many biblical references to the spiritual warfare being waged against mankind by dark forces in the world: "For our struggle is not against flesh and blood, but against the rulers, against the authorities, against the powers of this dark world and against the spiritual forces of evil in the heavenly realms."[41] The great Christian theologian and writer, C.S. Lewis, wrote *Screwtape Letters* to give insight into how these satanic forces might be going about their work in our lives. Many of his observations are outwardly humorous, but in all cases insightful and, ultimately, deadly serious.

---

[40] Wisdom of the Old Corps.

[41] Ephesians 6:12.

He writes from the point of view of a senior demon advising his nephew, who is new to the business of winning souls for his father (satan). Keep in mind that the *Enemy* is God, *Our Father* is satan, etc. So, in the following examples of *satanic* advice, we get an idea about how the principles of war might be used against us:

"Do what you will, there is going to be some benevolence, as well as some malice, in your patient's soul. The great thing is to direct the malice to his immediate neighbors whom he meets every day and thrust his benevolence out to the remote circumference, to people he does not know. The malice thus becomes wholly real and the benevolence largely imaginary."[42]

This advice illustrates OFFENSIVE, OBJECTIVE, and MANUEVER: Satan wants us to attack, always in the wrong direction.

"You ask me whether it is essential to keep the patient in ignorance of your own existence. That question . . . has been answered by the High Command. Our policy, for the moment, is to conceal ourselves. If any faint suspicion of your existence begins to arise in his mind, suggest to him a picture of something in red tights."[43]

---

[42] Lewis, C. S. *The Screwtape Letters: Letters from a Senior to a Junior Devil*. New York: MacMillan Paperbacks Edition, 1960, . p. 37.

[43] Ibid. p. 39-40.

This illustrates satan's use of SURPRISE: He uses total secrecy to keep us guessing as to his aims and even existence.

"He (God) has filled His world full of pleasures. There are things for humans to do all day long without His minding in the least—sleeping, washing, eating, drinking, making love, playing, praying, working. Everything has to be twisted before it's any use to us. We fight under cruel disadvantages. Nothing is naturally on our side."[44]

Satan can't comprehend SIMPLICITY: Joy and simple pleasures are anathema to everything he stands for.

The subjects of evil and spiritual warfare are difficult to conceive for many people, young and old, in the modern world. These subjects have certainly not been emphasized in the modern church. C. S. Lewis's observation that we tend to trivialize satan is more valid today than ever. Still, any person, Christian or otherwise, must observe that overt evil exists in the world and, moreover, seems to be extremely well organized. Terrorists, drug traffickers, the pornography industry all go about their businesses seemingly bent on ruining lives for profit or ideology. We also wonder about the source of bullying, bigoted, and violent behavior that we see spring forth from apparently ordinary people.

The apostle Paul, long ago, implored fellow believers to combat these and all other evil forces by

---

[44] Ibid. p. 112.

putting on the full armor of God, quoted below. I urge young Christians to use this armor in a positive way, as you go forth confident in your beliefs and understanding that you have a message the world needs desperately. We need to borrow the attitude of General George Patton, who, if addressing the spiritual war, might have said: "We won't win this or any war standing behind fixed fortifications!" We live in a fallen world that needs the presence of Christians. The spiritual battles have to be fought with a positive and joyful message, out in the open where we live and work. So onward, Christian soldiers!

Stand firm then, with the belt of truth buckled around your waist, with the breastplate of righteousness in place, and with your feet fitted with the readiness that comes from the gospel of peace. In addition to all this, take up the shield of faith, with which you can extinguish all the flaming arrows of the evil one. Take the helmet of salvation and the sword of the Spirit, which is the word of God. And pray in the Spirit on all occasions with all kinds of prayers and requests. With this in mind, be alert and always keep on praying for all the Lord's people. **Ephesians 6:14-18**

Courage is fear hanging on a minute longer.[45]

Appendix B

War on Women

This part is for women, although men might consider the benefit of understanding a woman's perspective on some important subjects. I introduced Lani in *A Special Note* at the beginning of this book to give her credit for much of the content. This part is more directly from her. She was a unique human being and the epitome of womanhood. She and I shared some confusion over where our culture seemed headed in the areas of sex and gender, as we were both of a simpler era when men were just men and women were women, and the French attitude prevailed: "Vive la difference!" Her advice for girls and young women may seem old fashioned to some, but nevertheless shaped our family for the better and is more relevant than ever for young women today.

---

[45] General George Patton.

There now seems to be quite a number of women who portray themselves and other women as victims of a male-dominated culture with a long history of repression. The phrase "war on women" has been introduced into the vocabulary, asserting that men are actively working to harm women economically and psychologically through unjust laws, sexual abuse, and/or discrimination in the workplace. These accusations have obvious utility for politicians and ideologues seeking to divide people into oppressor and victim categories, whether along the lines of race, income, or gender. Unfortunately, this alleged war has been made into a source of unnecessary discord between women and men. Lani never engaged in this line of thinking. She never considered herself a victim, physically or emotionally, and did her best to make sure that none of the women in her family ever let themselves become victims either.

While attending college at the Sorbonne in Paris, Lani held a summer job selling magazine subscriptions while traveling around Europe. On one notable occasion, she went into a large jewelry store in Geneva and asked to speak to the manager. After she was introduced and before she could say anything, the man announced that he was not going to purchase any magazines. Lani smiled at that and proceeded with her sales pitch, emphasizing the plight of men accompanying wives and girlfriends while jewelry-shopping. Before she left, the manager bought *all* her magazines— and then offered her a job! No, she never felt victimized or lacking in opportunity as a woman.

Lani was a woman and a warrior. She fought like a lioness for her husband, children, grandchildren, and family. She was a devoted Marine wife, patriotic American, and proud supporter of many veteran causes, such as Honor Flight, Heal our Patriots, and Fisher House. She was often outspoken and not known to back down from an issue she felt strongly about. She was also the most feminine and compassionate woman that I have ever known. She always urged young women, especially her own children and grandchildren, to be confident in themselves, to stand up and be counted, to be women of strength and courage.

Lani experienced a lot of jealousy from other girls growing up. She liked boys, was close to her older brother, and fit right in playing with him and his friends from an early age. She was extremely athletic and able to compete with the boys in every sport. Since she was also one of the most vivacious girls in school, she got a lot attention from the boys, with corresponding resentment from the girls. When she started dating the class president and captain of the football team in high school, the rumors started about what favors she was granting for the privilege. Considering this early form of bullying, her mother wisely counselled her to, "Hold your head high and be confident in who and what you are," and to not be cowed by false accusations and the opinions of others. This attitude became an important feature of Lani's character which she shared with her family and many others.

Lani was definitely of an older school like both our parents, who believed the highest role of a woman was in the family. There were times in our marriage when a second income did come in handy, and Lani provided this with her popcorn business and house-renovating ventures. Her main focus, however, was on the family, to the lasting benefit of our children and me. I tried to support and honor her in this role in every way possible. To me, there has never been a profession or position of a more important and exalted nature than that of mother.

As time passed in our marriage, we could both see the times changing, as more opportunities opened to young women and financial necessity required two working adults in many families. Considering this, Lani tried to counsel our own girls on balancing professional and family pursuits. She believed that the ability to support one's self is important; but she, nevertheless, believed that at some point a young woman, in spite of a professional interest, has a biological need for a stable, long-term relationship with the right man as the foundation of a family. She believed that casual sex and "living together" worked against this purpose. Although the culture seems to say otherwise, I believe that present-day psychological studies and the wisdom of our fore-bearers fully support this position.

Accordingly, Lani felt that young women should be careful with whom they invest their time and emotions.

For years, she had fended off her own arduous suitors, young and old, avoiding the physical relationships that most men strive for. She knew that wedding vows were, as they always have been, one of the few, if not only, real assurances a couple can give each other as to their long-term intentions. This stand becomes ever more difficult for a young woman today, as more and more contemporaries give themselves casually to men.

I wish Lani were here now to advise you further on this difficult issue. Sexual relations seem to get ever more complex, especially for females. I know she was particularly distressed to see girls let themselves be taken advantage of in these relationships. Her advice was to exercise due diligence in the selection of boyfriends, on the assumption that you can fall in love with just about anyone, once you become deeply involved. So, try to assess early and objectively what kind of person you are investing with your time. And, to quote Lani specifically, once on your own or out of college, when dating, "Never waste more than one year on any man." She saw too many five-year relationships end with a carefree man going on to greener pastures and an older woman starting over in the dating game. In fact, such splits are the rule rather than the exception, without the mutual commitment that forms the basis of marriage.

As I have already mentioned in Chapter 7, Lani took the biblical injunction, "Wives, submit to your husbands" seriously and gave me the tie-breaker in difficult family decisions. This did not occur often. Her everyday attitude was, "Larkin is the head of the family—but, I'm the neck!" Our family neck subtly and lovingly kept the head and the rest of the body pointed in the right direction.

One of Lani's mottoes for life was forged on the slopes of Mount Kilimanjaro, which she climbed at age sixty-nine with our daughter, Catherine Alexa. When I agreed to this expedition (as if I might have had veto power), I pictured it as a long, perhaps difficult, hike. I envisioned a well-marked and well-traveled trail to the top with plenty of support along the way. Well, this was not the actual situation. The "hike" was fraught with difficult climbing situations, high altitude, lack of oxygen, and moments of real danger. Day in and day out, Lani had to focus her efforts and will-power to keep going, telling herself and those with her over and over, "One step at a time!" This became a mantra for her when facing other difficult situations, whether physical or emotional. She believed that there are times when you shouldn't look too far ahead at all that has to be overcome. Just take care of what is directly in front of you.

Finally, I would like to share one insight into Lani's faith and its profound impact on others in her life. She became a Christian first in our family and is probably proud to be the first to actually be with Jesus. She saw a short film once called *The Music Box,* which told of a man who discovered a wonderful box full of music that poured out when opened. Unfortunately, the man feared losing the music and so chose to hide the box from others. The moral of the story is that we should share Jesus by opening our music boxes for others. This little story became an important metaphor for Lani and her theme for Christian living. There was never a more enthusiastic, one-on-one evangelist in God's kingdom than Lani, as she opened her music box for countless others.

The rest of this story occurred soon after Lani passed away on a sad evening in October 2017. My children and I had gathered in the living room, consoling each other when the grandkids came running down the hall, urging us to come quickly to the bedroom. There we heard the music box beside our bed, playing a minuet by Bach. Besides the fact that the music box had not worked in anyone's recent memory, it was playing joyfully, with the lid closed! This was the first of several miracles that assured us that even death could not hold back Lani's love and concern for her family. She had to open the music box for us one more time to make sure we knew that she was where she had always known she would be—and that heaven is for real.

To summarize Lani's advice for women:

PURPOSE: **SHARE** your music box.

MASS/OFFENSIVE: Be **STRONG.** Hold your **HEAD HIGH**.

OBJECTIVE: Take **ONE STEP** at a time.

SECURITY: Do your **DUE DILIGENCE** on boyfriends.

ECONOMY OF FORCE: When dating, never waste more than **ONE YEAR** on any man.

MANEUVER/SURPRISE: Vive **LA DIFFERENCE**!

UNITY OF COMMAND: Be the **NECK**.

SIMPLICITY: There is **NO** such thing for a woman.

> *A wife of noble character who can find? She is worth far more than rubies. Her children arise and call her blessed; her husband also, and he praises her: "Many women do noble things, but you surpass them all."* **Proverbs 31:10, 28-29**
>
> *He will wipe every tear from their eyes. There will be no more death or mourning or crying or pain, for the old order of things has passed away.* **Revelation 21:4**

Don't forget nothing.[46]

Appendix C

Military
(and related) Axioms

I am including in this appendix a collection of military axioms, or proverbs, to give further insight into the military attitude toward many situations and life in general. They are typically cynical, humorous, practical, and even irreverent. I have collected them over a lifetime and have included many in my devotional books. As stated in the beginning, most are apocryphal, and those with specific attribution have mostly been gathered from the internet, not from original sources. So, stand at ease, and *listen up*:

---

[46] Maj. Robert Rogers' Rule No. 1, *28 Rules of Ranging*, c. 1789.

Five second fuses last three seconds (rule of thumb for EOD technicians).

Bombs dropped from high altitude are very accurate. They always hit the ground (Grunt wisdom regarding close air support).

Keep calm and empty your magazine (military paraphrase of old school British wisdom).

Improvise, adapt, and overcome (motto of the modern Marine Corps).

Improvise, adapt, overcome—and redefine victory (old Corps addition to modern Marine Corps motto).

Assume: That which makes an ASS of U and ME (every-day reminder to Basic School students of every era).

Never interrupt your enemy when he is making a mistake (Napoleon Bonaparte).

He who fears being conquered is sure of defeat (Napoleon Bonaparte).

You've never been lost until you're lost at Mach 3 (wisdom of an SR-71 pilot with a malfunctioning navigation system over the North Pole).

Never eject over an area you just bombed (more aviator wisdom—for those employing air-to-ground ordnance).

If your attack is going really well, you're probably walking into an ambush (wisdom of the old Corps and useful advice for newlyweds).

No plan survives first contact with the enemy (an ancient and first principle of war).

Have a plan. Have a backup plan, since the first plan probably won't work (first rule of Command and Staff College).

Be polite. Be professional. But have a plan to kill everyone you meet. (advice for military personnel serving in the Middle East, popularized by FBI Director Robert Mueller and Gen. James Mattis, USMC).

Anything worth shooting is worth shooting twice (general advice for anyone carrying a firearm).

Decide to be aggressive enough, quickly enough (general advice for anyone threatened with bodily harm).

Do not attend a gunfight with a handgun whose caliber does not start with a "4" (small-arms instructor wisdom).

Only the dead have seen the end of war (George Santayana and, according to some, Plato).

Sweat (in training) *saves blood* (in combat) (Gen. Erwin Rommel).

Don't ever march home the same way (Rule no. 11, Rogers' Rangers).

Don't sleep beyond dawn (Rule no. 15, Rogers' Rangers).

If it moves, salute it. If it doesn't move, paint it (tongue-in-cheek (we hope) drill instructor advice to new recruits).

"Close" works in horse shoes and hand grenades (civilian wisdom based on a vague understanding of hand grenades).

Don't volunteer for anything (general military wisdom from the dawn of time, usually ignored by Marines, Soldiers, Sailors, and Airmen in times of extreme emergency).

You can't run an army without profanity; and it has to be eloquent profanity (Gen. George Patton).

Fixed fortifications are a monument to the stupidity of man. (Gen. George Patton).

You don't win a war by dying for your country. You win a war by making the other poor bastard die for his (George C. Scott in the movie *Patton*).

No combat-ready unit ever passed inspection. No inspection-ready unit ever passed combat (source unknown).

Incoming fire has the right of way (an oft heard catchy quote with unknown meaning).

Those who beat their swords into plowshares will plow for those who don't (sacrilegious "wisdom" of the old Corps).

Yea though I walk through the valley of the shadow of death I will fear no evil, because I'm the toughest s.o.b. in the valley (even more sacrilegious 'wisdom' of a fellow company commander in Vietnam, applicable only if accompanied by 200 fully armed Marines).

Expect to be bitten (or eaten) later by the things you sweep under the carpet now (frequent reminder from Col. Paul G. Graham, USMC, while commanding Marine Barracks, Washington, D.C.).

If the bubble gives you trouble, kick the baseplate (old school immediate action for leveling an 81mm mortar).

War is God's way of teaching Americans geography (Ambrose Bierce).

Tracers work both ways (wisdom from an old Corps machine gunner).

Two is one. One is none (modern Army logistical wisdom from Lt. Dan Rountree).

It's not the bullet with your name on it that you have to worry about. It's the one "to whom it may concern" (old Corps theology).

Don't worry if your time is up. Worry about being in a foxhole with someone else when HIS time is up (more old Corps theology).

Duty is the sublimest word in the English language (Gen. Robert E. Lee, quoted frequently by my father, and engraved on brass plaques in Citadel barracks).

Happiness is a byproduct of duty well performed (favorite saying of Eugenia Wood Norton Spivey, my mother).

Defeat can make you either bitter or better (another saying of my mother).

*Advance without coveting fame and retreat without fearing disgrace (*Sun Tzu*).*

Dulce et decorum est pro patria mori (Sweet and honorable it is to die for one's country). (Roman poet Horace, exhorting *others* to patriotic fervor, while not known to have come under direct fire himself.)

Si vis pacem, para bellum (If you wish for peace, prepare for war). (Publius Flavius Vegetius Renatus and motto of the Twenty-fourth Marine Regiment and origin of the word "parabellum," as used to describe certain types of ammunition and weapons.)

Any ship can be a minesweeper. Once. (unknown origin, likely from a surviving crewmember of one of the countless ships sunk by underwater mines in times of war and peace).

Whoever said the pen is mightier than the sword never encountered automatic weapons (Gen. Douglas MacArthur).

Courage is fear hanging on a minute longer (Gen. George S. Patton).

The best tank terrain is terrain without antitank weapons (Russian tank commander wisdom).

Always remember: pillage before you burn (Barbarian principle of war).

Draft beer, not people (Peace protester's sign).

Blow and go! (first rule of the road for Havana cab drivers, or last instruction before exiting the escape trunk of a submerged submarine).

www.ingramcontent.com/pod-product-compliance
Lightning Source LLC
Chambersburg PA
CBHW052144050526
44539CB00046B/1444